I wake up in the morning. Oh no, my hair's a mess!

But Daddy brushes out the knots to help me look my best.

Jump, stomp, run. Ouch, I hurt my toe!

But Daddy's got a band-aid ready to go.

I play with toys in my room. Uh oh, one broke in the bin.

But Daddy's quick to put it back together again.

We visit the park. Help, I've climbed too high!

But Daddy's always there to catch me in time.

open the markers. Yikes, colors all on the couch and the rug.

But Daddy cleans everything up with a little scrub-a-dub-dub.

Oh boy, my tummy! It's loud and it's rumbly!

But Daddy's made dinner so I won't go hungry.

We dip and we twirl as we dance before bed.

He whispers, "I love you," and kisses my head.

It's really dark and scary as he turns the lights out.

But Daddy's still close. There's nothing to worry about.

With Daddy around, I have everything I need.

He reminds me daily he'd do anything for me.

But what about Daddy? Who takes care of him?

I think it's someone he calls his Father, his Father in heaven.

Daddy is a kid too without a care in the world, just like me!

Because he has a Daddy who takes care of all of his needs

CPSIA information can be obtained
at www.ICGtesting.com
Printed in the USA
BVHW021259230721
612716BV00007B/246